Tot, the Thin Cub

By Sally Cowan

Tot was a thin cub.

Big Jag fed Tot.

Then Big Jag went off.

Mon hit nut shells on a log.

Mon had lots of nuts.

Tot did not sit in the den!

She got up on Mon's log.

"You are thin!" said Mon.
"Come and get some nuts."

Thud! Thud! Thud!

Tot smells a nut.

"No!" she said.

"The nuts smell bad!"

"Well, we can get figs!"
said Mon.

He looks at Tot.

"You can get them!"
said Mon. "You are thin.
The big log will not tip."

Tot got the figs!

Mon and Tot bit
some big figs.

"This fig is bad, too!"
said Tot.

"Well, what do thin little
cubs like?" said Mon.

Big Jag runs to get Mon ...
for Tot!

Mon went up and up
and up!

Big Jag can not get him.

CHECKING FOR MEANING

1. How did Mon break open the nuts? *(Literal)*

2. Why was Tot able to get the figs? *(Literal)*

3. Why didn't Tot like nuts or figs? *(Inferential)*

EXTENDING VOCABULARY

thin	Look at the word *thin*. How many sounds can you hear in this word? Which sound is changed to turn *thin* into *chin*?
thud	What is a *thud*? Is this a light sound or a heavy sound? What could you do to make a *thud*? Explain to students that this word is an example of onomatopoeia, that is, a word that imitates the sound made by the person or object in the text. Can you think of other examples of onomatopoeia? E.g. splat, pow, thump.
some	What do we mean by the word *some*? How many is *some*? What are other words we can use that have the same meaning? E.g. few, lots, any, several.

MOVING BEYOND THE TEXT

1. Why did Big Jag tell Tot to sit in the den?

2. What do baby cubs eat? What do they eat when they are older?

3. Why do you think Mon shared the nuts and figs with Tot?

4. What are some different types of big cats? E.g. lions, tigers, jaguars, leopards. What do they look like? What do they eat?

SPEED SOUNDS

| sh | ch | th | th | wh | qu | ph |

voiced   unvoiced

Then

thin

shells

them

Thud

This